Fire Engines

By E.S. Budd

SCHOLASTIC INC.

New York   Toronto   London   Auckland   Sydney
Mexico City   New Delhi   Hong Kong   Buenos Aires

For information regarding permission, write to:
The Child's World®, Inc.
P.O. Box 326
Chanhassen, Minnesota 55317

Photos: © 1998 David M. Budd Photography

ISBN 0-439-65046-1

Printed in the U.S.A.
First Scholastic printing, February 2004

Contents

On the Job

On the job, a fire engine helps put out fires. A fire engine carries big **hoses.**

Firefighters attach one end of a hose to a **fire hydrant.** The hydrant is like a big pipe. It gets water from the town's supply. The firefighters attach the other end of the hose to the engine's **pump.**

The pump can carry water to a **nozzle** on top of the truck. The firefighters use the nozzle to spray water at the fire.

Fire engines carry many important tools. Some tools help firefighters rescue people. Other tools help them put out fires. Tools are kept in **bins.**

Fire engines have bright lights.

They warn other drivers that

the engine is moving fast.

Fire engines also have **sirens** and noisy horns. They are very loud!

The engine is kept at the fire station.

It is always ready to go in an emergency.

Climb Aboard!

Would you like to see where the firefighters sit? The driver is called an **engineer.** Other firefighters sit in the back. It is very loud inside the truck. All the firefighters wear headphones to talk to each other. The engineer also has a **radio.** He uses it to talk to people at the fire station.

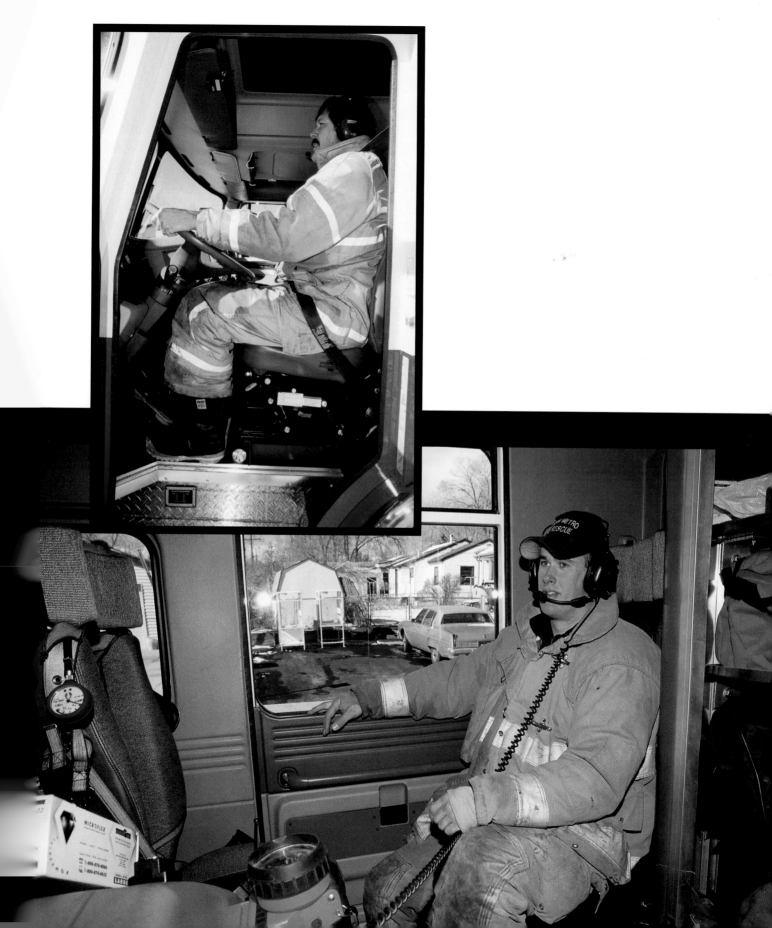

Up Close

The inside

1. The headphones

2. The steering wheel

3. The radio

The outside

1. The pump

2. The hose

3. The tool bins

4. The lights

5. The sirens

Glossary

bins (BINZ)
Bins are boxes inside the fire engine. The firefighters store tools inside the bins.

engineer (en-jin-EER)
An engineer is the driver of a fire truck. He or she sits in the front of the truck.

fire hydrant (FY-er HY-drent)
A fire hydrant is a pipe with a big spout. Firefighters use the engine to pump water from a hydrant.

hoses (HOZ-ez)
Hoses are long tubes that can move something wet. A firefighter attaches hoses to fire hydrants.

nozzle (NAWZ-el)
A nozzle is a tool attached to a hose or a pump. It helps spray water in the right direction.

pump (PUMP)
A pump is a device that lifts and moves something wet. Firefighters use pumps to get water from fire hydrants.

radio (RAY-dee-o)
A radio is a special machine on a fire engine. The engineer uses the radio to talk to people at the fire station.

sirens (SY-renz)
Sirens are horns that make very loud noises. A fire engine has sirens to warn people it is coming.